A WAY THROUGH THE WILDERNESS

A WAY THROUGH THE WILDERNESS

Experiencing God's Help in Times of Crisis

Paula Gooder

CHURCH HOUSE
PUBLISHING

Church House Publishing
Church House
Great Smith Street
London SW1P 3AZ

ISBN 978 0 7151 4188 5

Published 2009 by Church House Publishing

Cover design by Aubrey Design
Inside design by Hugh Hillyard-Parker, Edinburgh
Printed in the UK by CPI William Clowes Beccles NR34 7TL

Contents

Acknowledgements

In the writing of this course I am enormously indebted to a number of people for their advice and expertise. Kathryn Pritchard has offered me support and encouragement every step of the way from the conception of the idea to final submission of the manuscript and for that I am enormously grateful. Her mix of thoughtfulness, intuitive good sense and great sense of humour makes her a pleasure to work with.

In addition this course would not be what it is without the help of Terri Dauncey, who has provided unstinting, wise suggestions on how to improve both the content of the course as a whole and, in particular, the questions for group work. I am also grateful to Joanna Cox, Hannah Walpole and Penny Pierce and their respective house groups for being prepared to trial this course at an early stage in its development and for suggesting many helpful ways in which it might be improved.

How to use this course

Introduction

A trip into most bookshops will bring you face to face with a barrage of self-help books that seek to help us to find happiness, boost our self-esteem, relax and be less stressed. A lot of people find these books invaluable as they seek to face and work through the many challenges that life throws at them, and one of their greatest values is that they represent a refusal to accept that our lives should be made up only of unhappiness, stress and anxiety.

I have always felt, however, that self-help is somewhat bleak and lonely: a little like battling up a cliff face on your own. It is possible you'll make it to the top but the ascent will be hard going and somewhat precarious. For me the essence of the Christian message is that we don't have to do it alone. We are surrounded by other Christians who, to continue the metaphor, are scaling the same cliff face with us and who can offer advice on the best route to take, which points to avoid and even, when we slip, to pull on the rope and keep us from falling. Even more important than this, however, is the fact that God, who loves us, has let down a rope for us and wills us to catch hold of it. Of course we can go nowhere until we catch hold of it (that's the self-help element of our relationship with God) but when we do, we discover that we are not alone but are loved with an infinite love.

What then is the 'God-help' that God yearns to give us? The answers to this question could take up a number of books, let alone one short Bible study course. What this course seeks to do is to introduce you to one particular passage (Isaiah 40) that talks about God's comfort, and to help you to reflect on the help that God tried to give to his people in this passage. There are no easy answers but there is the assurance of God's love and care as we make our way through life and negotiate the good and the bad times.

It may seem an obvious thing to say but you do not need to be going through a bad time yourself to do this course. One of the values of courses such as this is that they help us to stock up life's tool kit. You may not need everything in your tool kit right now but there may come a time when you do. If you have been able to think through some of the issues before a crisis strikes (either a crisis of your own or that of someone you know and care for) then you may feel just that little bit more prepared than you would otherwise: a word of Scripture, a quotation, something wise said by a member of your group might come to mind when you need it most.

These five sessions focus, in turn, on five elements of help that God has offered and still offers to his people. They include:

- an encouragement to change and embrace the comfort that God offered
- a summons out into the wilderness to prepare to encounter God
- a challenge to become the messengers of the comfort that God seeks to give us
- an encounter with the God who created the world
- an encouragement to wait for God who will renew our fading strength with his own everlasting strength.

This is not the only help God wants to give us, but it's not a bad place to start.

Using this course

Your group

Some of the groups undertaking this course will be well established and know each other well; others may be relatively new or will have come together solely in order to undertake this course. It will be important to work out the needs of your group and to adapt the course material accordingly. The course seeks to weave a middle way between inviting people to share things about themselves (and people that they know) with the group and being more anonymous. For some groups this will be too intimate; for others not intimate enough. As a group leader you need to work out what works for your group and alter the tasks and questions accordingly.

This course is designed so that you can do the minimum of preparation and research in advance, but you do not have to use it all. Please feel free to edit the material as best fits your group and its needs. In particular use only the questions/discussion material that you need to use and ignore any material that does not fit the context of your group. The course includes far too many discussion questions for any one group. This is to give a variety of questions so that your group can take the material in the direction it finds most helpful. In the same way, if the group wants to take the discussion off in a direction not indicated by the course (and you feel that this will be beneficial for everyone concerned) then do feel free to let that happen. The timings given are also only guidelines to give you a sense of how long you have for each question. I have left the main chunk of time for discussion as a relatively long 45–50 minutes section because groups will differ on how long they want for each question.

Getting ready

At the start of each session is a section that tells you how to get ready. This includes a reflective piece I have written to get you into some of the issues arising out of the Bible passage you will be exploring. It would be good for group leaders to have read it before the session and group members are also recommended to read it in advance as it will enable them to tackle the passage and the questions at a deeper level. When we trialled this course some groups opted to read out the reflection in its entirety at the start of the session. This will add on about 5 minutes to the beginning of the session and you can decide whether you feel this would be beneficial for your group or not. If not, and people have not had time to read it in advance, the session will still work.

Following this is a list of things you will need to prepare in advance. Make sure you check the list in enough time to sort them for the group.

It would be good to play some music in the group – at the point indicated in the session – to give the people time to reflect on what they have been talking about. You can use any music you choose, though something meditative would be advisable! Either use CDs that you have already or, if you would like to buy something, try one of the following:

- *Taizé Chant*, St Thomas' Music Group, Margaret Rizza, 2006
- *Relax*, Classic FM, 2007
- *50 Instrumental Golden Hymns*, Kingsway, 2004 (or volume 2, 2005)
- *When Silence Falls*, Tim Hughes, Survivor, Kingsway, 2004
- *In Christ Alone*, Keith and Kristyn Getty, Kingsway Music, 2004
- *Acoustic Reflections*, Dan Wheeler Alliance Music, 2007.

At various points in the session, it is suggested that you play some music. If you are in a group that is comfortable with periods of silence, you may like to have silence instead of music; those groups, however, that are less familiar or comfortable with silence may find that music enables them to reflect more easily than sitting in silence.

The session

Getting started (10 minutes)

Each session will begin with a time of welcome, to help members leave behind what they've been doing and begin to focus upon the topic we are looking at.

You might like to begin by lighting the candle that acts as a focus point, to mark the formal start of the session and to say the opening course prayer.

Then there will be space to reflect on issues that have arisen from the previous session, before a brief topic to talk about in twos and threes to get the group into the theme for the week.

Hearing the word (5 minutes)

Then turn to the Bible passage for the week. Invite someone from the group to read the Bible passage out loud. I have re-translated each Bible passage with the aim of showing fresh insights into the passage. You can, if you find it helpful, invite the person reading the passage to read it from a published translation (like the NRSV or NIV or *Good News*) so that people have the chance to see what is different in this translation. Many of the passages you will look at in this particular course are quite short. You might like to read them out in two or three different versions to help you get into what the passage is saying. I have often left my own translation a little rough. This is deliberate so that you can see a bit more of what the Hebrew words were trying to get at. The purpose of it is not to produce a translation that you will like, take away, memorize and live with – but to help you to begin to ask questions about what the passage is really saying. Sometimes you need a translation that jars a little to help you to do this better.

Word highlights, etc. ...

After you have read the passage out there is a choice to be made that depends on your group and what the members want to do.

- You can either spend 5–10 minutes exploring the passage immediately and directly; *or*
- You can move straight on to Exploring the word, which explores the passage but does it slightly more obliquely.

The choice is for you and your group. Either way you will explore the passage: in one you will set out your own initial reactions to it before looking at the exploratory questions; in the other you will look at it *by* looking at the exploratory questions.

If you want to explore the passage in more detail you might find it helpful to remind people that they are not aiming for right answers or for profound insights but simply for their own reaction to what the passage says. They shouldn't shy away from stating the obvious – often the obvious is crucially important for helping us to get behind what is really going on in a passage. The following questions might also help you to explore the passage in more detail:

● Is there anything you particularly liked about this passage? Why do you like it?

● Did anything stand out for you from the passage?

● Did anything confuse you?

● How did it make you feel?

For those groups that want to look at the text itself, I have provided some additional information on key words in the passage (Word highlights ...) and in sessions 1–3 some historical and geographical information (History highlights, etc. ...). This is only for groups that want to know these kinds of thing (e.g. who was this text written to). If your group is not interested in these issues then do not pause over them – move directly on to the next section.

Exploring the word (45–50 minutes)

This is the major part of the session and encourages people to reflect on what the passage might be saying to them in their lives. The questions (marked with ⓠ) are designed to help people explore how the message of the passage might be applied to them. Use them as a springboard into the group's overall discussions.

Throughout the session you will find sections that contain material for further reflection (marked with ❸). These contain a range of quotations and stories relevant to the topic, which are in text boxes alongside the main material, as well as points for further consideration based on the biblical passages. You can bring these in to your discussion if you find them helpful but you can also ignore them if you find you have enough to talk about already.

Praying and reflecting/acting on the word (15–20 minutes)

Some weeks these sections are together as one section, other weeks they are split into different parts. The purpose of the praying, reflecting and acting on the word sections is to turn people's focus outwards from the group and to reflect

- on people and/or situations they know that are in need of prayer
- on what they have learnt personally and undertake to put it into action during the week.

Somewhat inevitably, given the subject matter of the course, the prayer sections often involve praying for people in need. It may be that these sections will need to include updates on those prayed for in previous sessions so that the group can continue to pray for people and/or situations over the five weeks of the course.

Closing (5 minutes)

At the end of each session there is time for people to write down one thing they may wish to take away with them from the session. (You could provide each member with a small notebook at the start of the course.) You may like to invite them to do so and possibly to share it out loud if they feel able to, or leave them to do it at home.

Round off the session using the responses and prayer provided (or indeed any other prayer that you may prefer to use).

Hints for facilitating your group

Many group leaders using this course will already be experienced in the leading and facilitating of groups. For those of you for whom this is your first time as a group leader or who have done it before but feel a little unsure about what you should be doing, here are some hints and tips for helping your group to go well.

Before people arrive

Check the chairs

Before people arrive do check that there are enough chairs for everyone and that each person will be able to see the other members of the group during the discussion. It is all too easy to focus on content and forget the chairs!

When to have refreshments

Also decide with the host of the group (or yourself if you are the host) whether you want to begin or end with coffee/tea/biscuits/other refreshments.

- The advantage of *beginning* with a drink is that people feel relaxed as they arrive; the problem is that it can then be hard to start the group on time. Decide an absolute start time and stick to it!

- The advantage of *ending* with a drink is that you don't have to worry about running on at the start of the group; the problem is that some people will have to dash away and may miss the opportunity to get to know the other members.

You can of course vary it from week to week (especially if the group is hosted by different people).

Setting a focal point

It can be good to have a focal point in the room (ideally on a table in the middle of the group) for people to look at during quiet moments or to stimulate people to think more visually about the topic you are discussing. This may involve using the items that you have brought for people to take away or you might like to use a picture, or some flowers in the centre of the room.

Even if you do not do that, try to have a candle (one relatively fat one will last you five weeks) as a way of signalling the beginning and end of the 'formal' part of the group.

At the start of the first session of the course

Even if you think that everyone knows each other, it is a very good idea to get people to introduce themselves so that no one feels left out. It can also be helpful for those who feel they 'know' people but cannot remember their names to be reminded of names, without the embarrassment of having to ask.

Some people love to have ice breakers at the start of a course – others loathe them and will do anything to avoid them, so be cautious about this. You might find that people's names are all that is needed at this point, until group members begin to feel more comfortable with each other.

When should the group end?

It is vitally important to agree an end time with the group, especially if you are meeting in the evening. People often will want to get home at the end of the session and need to feel confident that this will be possible every week. The content of the course is designed to last for 1 hour and 30 minutes, but you may want to stay on and talk for a bit at the end. The best idea is to agree a time at which people can leave if they need to, even if the informal chat of the group goes on after this time.

Facilitating a group

As a group leader, you do not need to know everything. In fact you may be relieved to discover that you do not, in fact, need to know anything! There are no right answers in this course. Your role is to enable people to explore the questions for themselves as clearly and thoughtfully as possible. It can be helpful, however, to come with questions and reflections prepared that will ease your group into discussion. It can also be helpful to think through in advance what you would say in response to each of the questions you are going to ask in the group. That way, if no one has any initial reflections, you can share yours as a way of helping them to express more clearly what they think.

It is important to value what people say (even if you violently disagree with it). Dismissing what someone says (especially in public) can mean that you destroy that person's self-confidence and it is important to encourage everyone in the group to value other people's contributions. If you can, find something positive to say about what someone has said – even if it is only thank you! If you want to disagree, try phrasing it as a question: 'Have you thought about ...? Or 'I wonder how that would affect ...?' or 'Does everyone agree or are there other ways of seeing this?'

If another member of the group is dismissive of what someone says, it is good to try to mediate by asking for more views: 'Person 1 thinks this ... Person 2 thinks that, are there any other ways of seeing it?' If you end up in the middle of a big row, it is probably a good idea to move on and agree to differ on that subject. However, it may be helpful for people if, at the end of the session, you offer to God in prayer the fact that you could not agree. This is a means of honouring the differing positions that exist within the group.

During the group discussion look out for which members speak during the group, how often they speak and how long they speak for.

● Some people will speak a lot.

This is fine provided that they do not 'hog' the discussion and make it difficult for others to speak or try to divert the discussion into something that they want to talk about but which is not the focus of the group's discussion. If you do have individuals who talk a lot then you may need to chip in to the middle of what they are saying and move the conversation on to enable other people to contribute or to turn attention back to the subject in hand.

If they do not get the hint, you might need to draw them on one side after the group and talk to them tactfully about moderating what they say so that others can also have a chance to join in.

- Some people may speak very little or not at all.

  It is worth going over the group in your mind after the event and working out whether there is anyone who hasn't spoken. Keep an eye on them and, if two sessions go by without them speaking at all, then you may like to direct a question at them during the next session to invite them to speak. If they still seem reluctant, don't press it, as they may not wish to speak out loud.

  It is important to recognize that some people are 'reflectors', in other words they will take it all in and go home and chew over what has been said. This is why it is important to give people the chance to say what they have been thinking about during the week. You may find that the quietest members of the group will return the following week with something profound to say and you need to give them the space to say it.

  Another point to be aware of is that, in the course, from time to time I suggest that people turn to their neighbour to talk but always give the option that this can also be done in the whole group. You will need to use your judgement on this:

- Some groups gel quickly and powerfully and prefer to do all their talking as a large group. The danger of this is that some people are squeezed out of the discussion and never get a chance to talk (or are so shy they don't feel able to speak in front of the whole group).

  Other groups have difficult personalities in them, which means that being asked to talk regularly in twos and threes can be a trial to the ones sitting next to them!

Keep your eye on what is going on and try to decide what will suit your group best.

The course at a glance

This course explores the help that God offers to his people in the remarkable, and often beautiful, chapter of Isaiah 40. Each session explores a different aspect of the comfort God seeks to offer us when we need it most.

Session

Embracing comfort

Based on Isaiah 40.1-2, this session explores what comfort is and what kind of comfort God seeks to offer to those who are in need.

Session

Stepping out

Based on Isaiah 40.3-5, this session looks at the theme of wilderness as a place not only of unhappiness but also of comfort..

Session

Becoming messengers

Based on Isaiah 40.6-11, this session reflects on the possibility that God wants us to become his messengers of comfort, even when we need that comfort for ourselves.

Session

Encountering God

Based on Isaiah 40.21-26, this session will help you to discuss God as creator and the message of hope that simply encountering God can give us.

Session

Receiving fresh strength

Based on Isaiah 40.27-31, this session will examine the beautiful passage from the end of Isaiah 40 that talks about rising up on wings like eagles, and reflect on what having God's strength in our lives might feel like.

Embracing comfort

At a glance

Getting started (10 minutes)

Introducing the course
Opening prayer
Getting to know each other

Hearing the word (5 minutes)

The passage: Isaiah 40.1-2
Word highlights – a few explanations about the passage
History highlights – a bit of historical background

Exploring the word (45–50 minutes)

Reflections, quotations and suggestions for group discussion focusing on:
● what is comfort?
● comfort and change
● comfort in the midst of crisis

Praying the word (10–15 minutes)

Prayer about the things that cause people in our modern world stress
and distress

Reflecting and acting on the word (5 minutes)

Invitation to write down the name of someone who is in need of comfort
and to pray for that person over the next week

Closing (5 minutes)

Time to reflect on what you want to take away from the session
Closing prayer

Embracing comfort

· ·

Getting ready

To prepare for the session, you need to read the passage for study (Isaiah 40.1-2) and the reflection on the passage below. We recommend that all group members read the reflection to help them focus their thoughts on the topic for this session but, if people don't have the time to do this, they will still be able to take part in the discussion.

(It can also be very helpful as a scene setter for the group if this material is read aloud near the start of the session.)

More on Isaiah 40.1-2

I don't know what the word comfort brings to your mind but for me it evokes a large comfy chair, a steaming cup of tea, probably some biscuits or cake, a friend to talk to and, if I am really upset, a box of tissues to mop up my tears. Your ideas of finding comfort may be completely different – perhaps a long walk in the countryside, or some time by yourself, maybe some music or something else entirely. I don't think I'm entirely alone, however, in associating comfort both with 'being comfortable' and with 'being soothed'. So-called 'comfort food' – pasta, stodgy puddings, chocolate and the like – and the notion of 'retail therapy' – going shopping and buying new things as an outward means of making our inner selves feel better – both combine that idea of soothing our inner selves with something physical.

When God calls out for someone to comfort his people here, however, a different form of comfort seems to be in mind. Although the meaning of the word comfort isn't entirely clear, it does seem to be quite closely associated with the idea of active change. So, for example, in Isaiah 51.3 the promise is given that God will 'comfort' the waste places and the wildernesses and make them like Eden. What this means is that God will change them from barren places to a beautiful and fertile garden. In the same way God seeks to comfort his people by changing them from people who are overwhelmed with despair and hopelessness into a people of vision and hope. Often we think of God as a bit like a firefighter or paramedic who, when asked, will come and save us while we lie there helplessly awaiting rescue. The image of comfort here suggests that God has a different model in mind that involves our doing something as well. Here God is more like a spiritual companion or even, in modern terms, a life coach, who expects us to work with him to find comfort.

God's comfort, therefore, is a comfort that doesn't just soothe and make us feel better. God's comfort draws us beyond our current situation and demands that we change the way we look at things. It is easy, when we are in situations of despair, to become stuck, helpless and unable to move forwards or backwards. We become bogged down in ourselves and the hopelessness of our situation. God's message of comfort was one that drew the people of Israel onwards out of their current despair and into the future that God had in mind for them. God still seeks to comfort us and to offer us a way out of our 'stuckness'. It is a way out that brings hope, new life and the comfort for which we yearn but now, as then, also demands that we move beyond ourselves into a situation that can embrace the comfort God yearns so much to give us.

Things you will need for the group

- A candle
- *Either* a flip chart and pens *or* enough paper and felt pens for people to have one each
- Some music to play
- Music-playing equipment
- Small piece of blank card (ideally) or, if not, paper for people to take away and pens

Embracing comfort

Getting started   10 minutes

Introducing the course

As this is the first week, spend five minutes introducing the course. You might like to draw people's attention to:

● the course 'At a glance' page so they can see the overview of the different sessions – spend a few minutes talking the group through the shape of the course so that they know what to expect in the weeks to come.

● the recommendation that the group members read the 'More on Isaiah ...' section for each session in 'Getting ready' to help them think their way in to the each week's session.

This course explores the help that God offered to his people at a particular time in their history when they were in great need of comfort. The God who yearned to comfort them then still yearns to comfort us today in all our difficulties, stresses and anxieties and we can learn a lot about what this comfort is like from the words of Isaiah 40. Over the course of the next five sessions, we will explore five key aspects of the comfort that God yearns to give us.

Opening prayer

Light a candle, then open the study with the course prayer – either use this one or one of your own.

God of all comfort,
where we are stuck, release us,
where we have given up hope, inspire us,
where we focus only on ourselves,
help us to see the needs of others;
transform us by your Spirit to be the people
you have called us to be,
spreading your love and proclaiming your
presence throughout the world.
We ask this through your son,
our Saviour Jesus Christ.
Amen.

Getting to know each other

As this is the first session, spend five to ten minutes introducing yourselves to each other (see the section headed 'At the start of the first session of the course' in the Introduction, page 7).

Hearing the word   5 minutes

Ask someone in the group to read out the passage: Isaiah 40.1-2 (as the passage is so short you could, if you like, read it in more than one version, or read it slowly and thoughtfully to give people time to think about it more).

> **v. 1**   Comfort, comfort my people says your God,
>
> **v. 2**   Speak to the heart of Jerusalem and cry out to her
>   that her warfare is completed,
>   that her punishment has been accepted,
>   that she has received from the hand of the Lord double for
>   all her sins.

Word highlights

If you have not had time to consult the introduction, read pages 4–5 for guidance on the purpose of Word and History highlights and how you might (or might not) use them in your group.

● **v. 1** – The command 'comfort' here is, in Hebrew, plural. This is something that can't be communicated well in modern English (though the King James Version does by translating it 'Comfort ye' – in King James English 'thee' is singular and 'ye' is plural). What this means it that God is not just telling one prophet to do this job but is calling out to find anyone who is willing to go out and comfort his people.

● **v. 2** – The usual translation of 'speak tenderly' doesn't quite communicate the whole meaning of the passage here: God's command is to speak to the heart of Jerusalem. This does involve being tender but also speaking directly to the heart of Jerusalem and telling her what she most needs to hear; speaking to someone's heart does not always involve being tender.

Those who are to comfort Jerusalem are to cry out (a bit like a town crier) that the bad times are now over and Jerusalem is to look forward to a different and more hopeful future

History highlights

Reading Isaiah can be very confusing because the events that he was addressing seem to jump around a lot. At one point he is promising doom for the people and at another comforting them. If it would help you to know more of the history then read on; if not, then skip to the next section.

It seems likely that this section of Isaiah (chapters 40–55) was written in a period later than the first section of the book (chapters 1–39). The first 39 chapters of Isaiah mention kings and events that can all be dated to the eighth century BC, whereas chapters 40–55 bring in new characters, particularly King Cyrus II of Persia (also known as Cyrus the Great, mentioned in Isaiah 45.1), who ruled from 559–529 BC.

Cyrus was destined to play a major role in the lives of the people of Judah. When he came to power a large number of Judeans lived in exile in Babylon, taken there by the Babylonian army 50 to 60 years earlier. Cyrus overturned the Babylonian policy, freed all captives and announced that they could go home. Here, the prophet Isaiah is trying to get the people ready for this brighter future, so that when it comes they will be prepared for all that it may bring.

Timeline

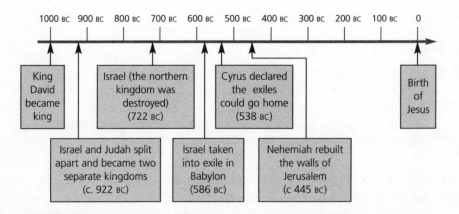

Exploring the word

What is comfort?

In Isaiah 40.1, God calls out for someone to comfort his people, but what does this mean?

Spend 5–10 minutes either discussing or jotting down on a large piece of paper or flip chart (or both) what the word 'comfort' means to you. Use the dictionary definitions given below, if you like, to help you explore various aspects of the word:

comfort

VERB

1 to soothe, console, or reassure; bring cheer to.

2 to make physically comfortable.

3 to aid; support or encourage.

NOUN

4 relief in affliction; consolation; solace: e.g. 'Her presence was a comfort to him.'

5 a feeling of relief or consolation: e.g. 'Her forgiveness afforded him great comfort.'

6 a person or thing that gives consolation: e.g. 'She was a great comfort to him.'

7 a cause or matter of relief or satisfaction: e.g. 'The patient's recovery was a comfort to the doctor.'

8 a state of ease and satisfaction of bodily wants, with freedom from pain and anxiety: 'He is a man who enjoys his comfort.'

9 something that promotes such a state: 'His wealth allows him to enjoy a high degree of comfort.'

10 chiefly Midland and Southern US, a comforter or quilt.

11 *obsolete.* strengthening aid; assistance.

Comfort and change

In the Old Testament, the word comfort has another, added dimension: that of change. For example elsewhere in Isaiah, the prophet says: 'For the Lord will comfort Zion; he will comfort all her waste places, and will make her wilderness like Eden, her desert like the garden of the Lord; joy and gladness will be found in her, thanksgiving and the voice of song' (51.3, NRSV). This seems to suggest that Israel's waste places, wilderness and desert will be comforted *by* being changed. A similar point may be being made here when God calls for someone to 'speak to the heart of Jerusalem'. This seems to imply that Jerusalem needs to hear a message that speaks the truth, as God's sees it, into their hearts.

Change seems to me to be an important aspect of comfort. Often our own understanding of comfort can imply a sense of feeling better while we remain as we are. In Isaiah there seems to be an active expectation that, if we want to receive comfort, we need to change. When John the Baptist began his ministry, his message was very similar. The word 'repent' literally means 'to change your mind'. John the Baptist was calling for people to change so that when Jesus came they could recognize him for who he was.

Comfort the disturbed and disturb the comfortable.

Anon

In those days John the Baptist appeared in the wilderness of Judea, proclaiming, 'Repent, for the kingdom of heaven has come near.' This is the one of whom the prophet Isaiah spoke when he said,

'The voice of one crying out in the wilderness:

"Prepare the way of the Lord, make his paths straight."'

Matthew 3.1-3

In religion, as in war and everything else, comfort is the one thing you cannot get by looking for it. If you look for truth, you may find comfort in the end: if you look for comfort, you will not get either comfort or truth – only soft soap and wishful thinking to begin with and, in the end, despair.

C. S. Lewis, Mere Christianity

Look (or think) back to your definitions of comfort. Does thinking about comfort in terms of change alter your definitions of comfort in any way?

Discuss one or more of the following questions:

● How might helping people to see the world differently comfort them?

● How does God speak into the heart of your situation today?

Comfort in the midst of crisis

One of the things that irritates me most when I am upset is for people to try to comfort me by saying 'it's all right'. Of course, it is not all right, if it were I wouldn't be upset!

God's message is not quite 'it is all right' but 'it will be all right'. God has declared the end of warfare, punishment and suffering for the people – even if they can't see the fruits of that quite yet. God does not downplay our current upset by telling us everything is fine when it is not, but asks us to lift our eyes and look beyond our current situation into the future that he yearns to give us. A very similar theme runs through much of the New Testament: we can bear our current difficulties because we know that God will save us in the future. It is this kind of thinking that lies behind this quotation from 1 Peter.

> '[you,] who are being protected by the power of God through faith for a salvation ready to be revealed in the last time. In this you rejoice, even if now for a little while you have had to suffer various trials.'
>
> *1 Peter 1.5-6*

The message in the passage from Isaiah is that the exiles are to be comforted *before* anything has really changed. This comfort that the people are to receive is based on the promise that their circumstances will change, even if they haven't yet.

Remember your word to your servant,
in which you have made me hope.
This is my comfort in my distress,
that your promise gives me life.

Psalm 119.49-50

It takes two to speak the truth:
one to speak, and another to hear.

Henry David Thoreau

Discuss one or more of the following questions:

● Can we still be comforted when our situation looks helpless?

● Can you think of a point in your life when, although circumstances remained difficult, things began to feel better and you began to turn a corner? What happened to enable this to take place?

Praying the word   10–15 minutes

The people to whom this prophecy was addressed were in dire need of comfort: their city had been destroyed, their leaders taken away to another country and, probably worst of all, God seemed to have abandoned them. There seemed to be no hope at all for the future. People today are in a similar need of comfort but the causes of their distress are more varied.

Spend five minutes talking about the major causes of the stress and distress that affect the people who live and work near you. Here you can either share stories of particular people that you know or give general examples of the kinds of stress and distress that people suffer today.

Spend time in silence or out loud bringing to God in prayer the people or things that you have just been talking about.

Reflecting and acting on the word 5 minutes

> ### Note on action
> Over the course of the next five weeks, each week you will
> have something to take home with you to pray about and
> think about more. You might like to make a space at home for
> these things. Some people like to have a prayer corner with a candle
> and a Bible, or it could be a shelf ... anywhere really but somewhere that
> you will remember to return to during the next five weeks.

This passage explores the idea of comfort and what God's comfort might be like.

While some music plays, write down on a piece of card or paper (given to you by
the group leader) someone or something for whom/which you will pray for the
next week.

This might be someone known to you who is in need. It might be someone or
some people you have heard about in the news who are in particular need of
comfort. It might even be something, like unemployment or famine, that affects
a large group of people, which you would like to hold in your heart before God
over the course of the next week.

Once you have written something down, hold the paper while you sit and begin
to pray now. Remember to take the paper home and use it in your prayers
during the week.

Closing   5 minutes

> The first aspect of God's help in a time of crisis to which Isaiah
> draws our attention is the need for us to embrace the
> comfort that God yearns to give us, a comfort that involves
> our changing in order to receive it.

Write down in your notebook something that you want to take away.
It might be a quote, something someone said or something you want to
think about some more.

As an end to your session, pray the following words together, ending with the prayer below.

The person leading this part (who doesn't need to be the group leader) should say the words in regular type and the group should say the words in bold:

In our despair and hopelessness
God comforts us
When we are bogged down and stuck
God comforts us
When we cannot see which way to go
God comforts us
When the way ahead seems dark and difficult
God comforts us
and draws us on to be the people he is calling us to be.
Amen.

O Christ Jesus,
when all is darkness
and we feel our weakness and helplessness,
give us the sense of your presence,
your love, and your strength.
Help us to have perfect trust
in your protecting love
and strengthening power,
so that nothing may frighten or worry us,
for, living close to you,
we shall see your hand,
your purpose, your will through all things.
Amen.

St Ignatius of Loyola

At the end of the prayer – if you lit a candle blow it out to signal the end of the group.

Stepping out

At a glance

Getting started (15 minutes)

Opening prayer
Recap on last week
Thinking about wilderness

Hearing the word (5 minutes)

The passage: Isaiah 40.3-5
Word highlights – a few explanations about the passage
Geography highlights – a bit of historical background

Exploring the word (45–50 minutes)

Reflections, quotations and suggestions for group discussion focusing on:
● wilderness in the Bible
● physical, emotional and spiritual wildernesses

Praying, reflecting and acting on the word (15 minutes)

Reflect on wilderness experiences of your own and commit to pray for those
of another member of your group

Closing (5 minutes)

Time to reflect on what you want to take away from the session
Closing prayer

Stepping out

Getting ready

To prepare for the session, you need to read the passage for study (Isaiah 40.3-5) and the reflection below on the passage. We recommend that all group members read the reflection to help them focus their thoughts on the topic for this session but, if people don't have the time to do this, they will still be able to take part in the discussion.

More on Isaiah 40.3-5

I will never forget my first experience of desert. I was in Israel at the time and had driven out to Masada, the infamous place where the Jews made their last stand against the Roman army. I stood on the top of Masada and looked out over mile upon mile of wilderness. It was summer. The air was hot. Nothing moved as far as the eye could see, apart from the heat shimmering up from the sand. The land was desolate but I was surprised to discover that within me were two emotions. The first was the one I expected, and bordered on terror. When you are there looking at it, the danger of the desert is hard to avoid. This was truly a wild place – a wilderness – where nature was easily stronger than humanity. Alongside this emotion, however, was a second more surprising feeling. It was a sense of spaciousness and of healing – that here was a place where I could find peace.

The exiles would have been all too familiar with the desert. There is lots of desert in Judah where they came from, but it is also worth remembering that their parents – and maybe even their grandparents – would have trekked across the Arabian desert in the desolate journey to captivity under the Babylonians. Isaiah's message that the preparations for the good times to come must take place in the wilderness may well have struck them as very odd indeed. It certainly seems odd to us. When you are stressed, upset and desolate, surely the last thing you should do is to go into the wilderness. My instinct is the opposite: to stay at home, preferably under the duvet, in comfort and safety. Yet the message seems to be that the comfort that God yearned to give the people in Isaiah 40.1 will come if they can go out into the wilderness and prepare for it.

The idea that lies behind this comes from Ezekiel, where God was declared to have abandoned the Temple – the place where he dwelt in the midst of his people – on his angelic chariot (Ezekiel 11.22-25). Here Isaiah is telling them to build a huge motorway in the middle of the desert so that God's chariot could return. I suspect, however, that this is not the only reason why the exiles are told to go out to the desert. The biblical writers knew the spiritual power of the desert, which, as well as being desolate, was a place for new birth and refreshment. God seems to be saying that, in order to find the comfort we crave, we have to do the opposite of what our instinct dictates; rather than staying still and seeking comfort by being passive we are to journey into the unknown and somewhat terrifying wilderness.

This message can appear to have a slightly uncaring, stiff-upper-lip quality about it: 'don't wallow, get out there and sweat a bit and you'll feel better'. This is not what I think is meant. The first thing to notice is that the exiles are not in their first phase of grief (nor even the second, third or fourth phases) but have been in exile for about 60 years. The comfort offered here is to stop them being stuck in their grief; not to stop them grieving in the first place. The second thing to notice is that going into the wilderness was not 'self-help' but 'God-help'. The aim of doing it was to encounter the living and loving God. Going into the wilderness allows us to leave the clutter of the everyday and to encounter the living and loving God.

Things you will need for the group

- A candle
- *Either* a flip chart and pens *or* enough paper and felt pens for people to have one each
- Some music to play
- Music-playing equipment
- A small stone or pebble for each member of the group to take away
- Map of Judah showing position of Jerusalem, Dead Sea and River Jordan (from the back of a Bible perhaps)

2

Stepping out

Getting started

15 minutes

Opening prayer

Light a candle, then open the study with the course prayer – either use this one or one of your own

God of all comfort,
where we are stuck, release us,
where we have given up hope, inspire us,
where we focus only on ourselves,
help us to see the needs of others;
transform us by your Spirit to be the people
you have called us to be,
spreading your love and proclaiming your
presence throughout the world.
We ask this through your son,
our Saviour Jesus Christ.
Amen.

Recap on last week

Last week's session explored God's yearning to comfort us by helping us to change and see the world differently.

Now, take five minutes to share any questions, observations or reflections that you have been thinking about comfort this week.

Turning to this week

This week we will be thinking about wildernesses and experiences of being in the wilderness.

As a group, take five to ten minutes to discuss what the word 'wilderness' brings into your mind.

- What is a wilderness like?

- What does it have in it? What doesn't it have in it?

- Is it a positive or negative word in your mind?

Hearing the word   5 minutes

Ask someone in the group to read out the passage: Isaiah 40.3-5 (again you might like to ask people to read this passage in more than one version so that you can hear the different emphases of different versions).

v. 3	A voice sounding 'In the wilderness, clear a path for the Lord; in the desert make a straight road for our God.
v. 4	Every valley shall be lifted up and every mountain and hill made low. The steep bits will be made into a plateau, and the rough bits into a plain.
v. 5	And the Lord's glory will be revealed, and all living beings will see it together, because the mouth of the Lord has spoken.'

Word highlights

- **v. 3** – We are so used to this passage that its incongruous command can pass us by. What the voice is asking for here is a motorway across the middle of the desert to aid God's return.

- **v. 4** – It sounds a little odd to ask for the ground to be flattened (which is effectively what the voice is asking for in verse 4) but this begins to make sense when we understand this passage in the light of the prophet Ezekiel. In Ezekiel 11, the prophet saw God leaving the Temple in his divine chariot: flattening the ground and making a motorway in the wilderness prepares for God's chariot to return. The people are to go out and make it possible for God to come back.

Geography highlights

Have a quick look at a map. It can help to locate precisely which desert we are talking about here.

The people of the exile probably lived on the banks of the river Euphrates (or one of its tributaries) in Babylon. Between Babylon and Judah lies the Arabian desert, and it is almost certainly this desert that is being referred to in this passage.

This desert runs all the way up to the east side of the river Jordan and was important in the mind of the people of God because that was the place from which they had originally entered the Promised Land. So this passage is more than just a call to help God back, but is marking a new Exodus experience in which the people leave captivity and re-enter the Promised Land. In short, it is a clean slate; the chance to start again.

Exploring the word   45–50 minutes

Wilderness in the Bible

Spend some time thinking about the theme of wilderness in the Bible and explore one or more of the following questions:

● What do you notice about the different reasons for which people go into the wilderness?

● Are any of these experiences good experiences? Are any of them bad? What do you think makes them good or bad?

● Notice that some of these experiences of wilderness are long term (for example the people who left Egypt were in the wilderness for 40 years). What difference does being in the wilderness for a long time make? Does it affect how easy it is for us to find comfort?

Either use the occasions you bring to mind or, if you can't think of any, use some of or all the ones on pages 31–32.

The wilderness wanderings after the Exodus

Key words are in bold.

And the Lord's anger was kindled against Israel, and he made them wander in the **wilderness** for **forty years**, until all the generation that had done evil in the sight of the Lord had disappeared.

Numbers 32.13

Surely the Lord your God has blessed you in all your undertakings; he knows your going through this great **wilderness**. These **forty years** the Lord your God has been with you; you have lacked nothing

Deuteronomy 2.7

Remember the long way that the Lord your God has led you these **forty years** in the **wilderness**, in order to humble you, testing you to know what was in your heart, whether or not you would keep his commandments. He humbled you by letting you hunger, then by feeding you with manna, with which neither you nor your ancestors were acquainted, in order to make you understand that one does not live by bread alone, but by every word that comes from the mouth of the Lord

Deuteronomy 8.2-3

Elijah after the battle with the prophets of Baal

Then Jezebel sent a messenger to Elijah, saying, 'So may the gods do to me, and more also, if I do not make your life like the life of one of them by this time tomorrow.' Then he was afraid; he got up and fled for his life, and came to Beer-sheba, which belongs to Judah; he left his servant there.

But he himself went a day's journey into the **wilderness**, and came and sat down under a solitary broom tree. He asked that he might die: 'It is enough; now, O Lord, take away my life, for I am no better than my ancestors.' Then he lay down under the broom tree and fell asleep. Suddenly an angel touched him and said to him, 'Get up and eat.' He looked, and there at his head was a cake baked on hot stones, and a jar of water. He ate and drank, and lay down again. The angel of the Lord came a second time, touched him, and said, 'Get up and eat, otherwise the journey will be too much for you.' He got up, and ate and drank; then he went in the strength of that food forty days and forty nights to Horeb the mount of God.'

1 Kings 19.2-8

After this he heard the still small voice of God.

Jesus in the wilderness

Then **Jesus** was led up by the Spirit into the **wilderness** to be tempted by the devil. He fasted forty days and forty nights, and afterwards he was famished.

Matthew 4.1-2

Jesus withdraws to pray after hearing the death of John the Baptist

Now when **Jesus** heard this, he **withdrew** from there in a boat to a deserted place by himself. But when the crowds heard it, they followed him on foot from the towns.

Matthew 14.13

Physical, emotional and spiritual wildernesses

Exploring the desert places

The wilderness that Isaiah is talking about here is an actual place. People often go into a 'wilderness', whether it be the mountains, the desert, or somewhere far away from everything that they know to find themselves, to gain a new direction for their lives or to encounter God. This is what caused people like the desert fathers (hermits who lived in the desert near Egypt from around the third century AD in an attempt to develop a deeper relationship with God) to spend most of their lives in the desert.

> The Promised Land always lies on the other side of wilderness.
>
> *Havelock Ellis*

> Wilderness is not a luxury but a necessity of the human spirit.
>
> *Edward Abbey*

As a group discuss one or more of the following questions:

- If you needed to get away from it all and go to a 'wilderness' place, where would you go? If you can, share with the group an occasion when withdrawing to a wilderness place helped you see the way ahead.

- If you are unable to go away to a physical wilderness, how might you find an inner wilderness that has the same effect? What would you need to do to help you find such an inner wilderness?

Wildernesses within

Wildernesses are not always physical. Some are internal, emotional or spiritual places.

The wilderness being referred to by Isaiah here is a *profitable* wilderness, one in which help can be found for the future. There are other kinds of wilderness that are unremittingly desolate, in which there is no salvation to be found at all.

> Generally speaking, a howling wilderness does not howl: it is the imagination of the traveller that does the howling.
>
> *Henry David Thoreau*

> You have to leave the city of your comfort and go into the wilderness of your intuition. What you'll discover will be wonderful. What you'll discover is yourself.
>
> *Alan Alda*

> Save me, O God, for the waters have come up to my neck.
> I sink in deep mire, where there is no foothold;
> I have come into deep waters, and the flood sweeps over me.
> I am weary with my crying; my throat is parched.
> My eyes grow dim with waiting for my God.
>
> *Psalm 69.1-3*

As a group discuss the following question:

- There are times when our emotional wilderness seems to be without hope. What is the difference between a wilderness in which you can find hope and one that is simply desolate?

Praying, reflecting and acting on the word
15 minutes

With music playing, hand a stone to each person in the group.

Sit in silence for a while, holding the stone given to you and call to mind any situation past or present when you have experienced a 'wilderness time'. Bring this experience before the God of comfort.

After a few minutes, split into twos (or threes) and swap stones. You may either do so in silence or, if you feel able, share with the other members of the group what caused this experience. Take the other person's stone home with you and undertake to pray for them for the rest of the week.

After this, either in your twos and threes or in the group as a whole, turn your attention to the wider community and world. Call to mind situations around the nation and the world that might be described as 'wilderness' times and offer these to God in prayer.

Closing
5 minutes

The second aspect of God's help in a time of crisis to which Isaiah draws our attention is the need for us to step out into the wilderness because, sometimes, it is there that peace and wholeness are to be found.

Write down something that you want to take away. It might be a quote, something someone said or something you want to think about some more.

As an end to your session, pray the following words together, ending with the prayer on the next page.

The person leading this part (who doesn't need to be the group leader) should say the words in regular type and the group should say the words in bold:

God of oasis and of desert
Give us glimmers of your glory
When life seems desolate and lonely
Give us glimmers of your glory
When the way is tough and the going is hard
Give us glimmers of your glory
In the wilderness places of our lives
Give us glimmers of your glory
and then bring us home.
Amen.

May the peace of the Lord Christ go with you,
wherever he may send you.
May he guide you through the wilderness,
protect you through the storm.
May he bring you home rejoicing
at the wonders he has shown you.
May he bring you home rejoicing
once again into our doors.
Amen.

Northumbria Community

At the end of the prayer – if you lit a candle blow it out to signal the end of the group.

Becoming messengers

· ·

At a glance

Getting started (15 minutes)

Opening prayer
Recap on last week
Thinking about becoming the messenger of God's comfort

Hearing the word (5 minutes)

The passage: Isaiah 40.6-11
Word highlights – a few explanations about the passage
People highlights – who is Isaiah talking to in his prophecy?

Exploring the word (45–50 minutes)

Reflections, quotations and suggestions for group discussion focusing on:
● finding and offering comfort
● comfort and experience
● the presence of God

Praying the word (5 minutes)

Pray for those in need of comfort

Reflecting and acting on the word (10 minutes)

Commit yourself to offer support to someone you know who is most in need
of comfort at the moment

Closing (5 minutes)

Time to reflect on what you want to take away from the session
Closing prayer

Becoming messengers

Getting ready

To prepare for the session, you need to read the passage for study (Isaiah 40.6-11) and the reflection on the passage below. We recommend that all group members read the reflection to help them focus their thoughts on the topic for this session but, if people don't have the time to do this, they will still be able to take part in the discussion.

More on Isaiah 40.6-11

There is nothing like having to teach a subject to ensure that you know it really well. I remember, when I first started lecturing, that sense, bordering on panic, when I got up to speak and people listened and wrote down what I said. What if I was wrong? What if what I said was inaccurate? That fear made me work harder than I had ever done before. In my first year of teaching I learnt and internalized far more than I had ever done in years and years of being a student. Being the messenger, announcing something with conviction and clarity, requires us first to learn it deeply, to comprehend it, to clarify it to ourselves and then to proclaim it.

One of the most striking features of Isaiah 40.1-31 is the fact that those who needed comfort in verse 2, are now the messengers in verse 9. Jerusalem is now the one who is to bring a message of good news to the whole of Judah. A part of Jerusalem's journey to recovery was the best learning experience of all – to become the messenger announcing God's presence to its neighbours. This must have been incredibly effective. I remember a number of years ago a friend of mine died and I was knocked sideways by it for a while. Various people tried to comfort me but none of this was of any help until I talked to someone who had recently lost her husband, who spoke about her experience and how she was slowly learning, not to come to terms with it, but to live each day one step at a time. Comfort comes best from those who know the darkest, deepest despair because we know that they, of all people, know what they are talking about.

Zion/Jerusalem (Zion is simply another way of talking about Jerusalem) is the ideal one to comfort the cities of Judah because its people would know what the cities of Judah most needed to hear. They are the ones who are called to lift up their voices in encouragement to the people who lived in Judah outside Jerusalem, and their message is to be a simple one: 'Look, your God is coming' (see 40.9-10). The people who only a few verses before were in desperate need of comfort themselves are now to be the ones who are pointing out God's coming presence to others. Paradoxically, part of the comfort they will receive seems to be to offer comfort to others. Comfort will not be achieved by sitting there waiting for it but by picking up the message of God's presence and passing it on.

This assurance of God's presence is not based on emotion or our ability to feel God's presence, but on trust in God. Isaiah is prophesying here at a stage when no one has seen any evidence of God's return whatsoever apart from the simple fact that God has promised it. Jerusalem is called upon to trust this word (a word that 40.8 tells us lasts for ever and ever) not only for itself but to trust it so much that it becomes its messenger to those around it.

There comes a time, in the midst of despair, when we can find comfort not by bedding down, expecting others to come to us with a message of hope, but by taking a leap of faith and going outwards, reaching out to people around us and lifting their eyes to the horizon saying: 'Look, your God *is* coming.' There comes a time when we are asked not just to hear and receive a message of comfort but to become its messenger.

Things you will need for the group

- A candle
- Some music to play
- Music-playing equipment
- An envelope and piece of paper or postcard for each of the group

Becoming messengers

Getting started

Opening prayer

Light a candle, then open the study with the course prayer – either use this one or one of your own

> God of all comfort,
> where we are stuck, release us,
> where we have given up hope, inspire us,
> where we focus only on ourselves,
> help us to see the needs of others;
> transform us by your Spirit to be the people you have called us to be,
> spreading your love and proclaiming your presence throughout the world.
> We ask this through your son,
> our Saviour Jesus Christ.
> Amen.

Recap on last week

Last week's session explored the idea of wildernesses that bring peace as well as 'wildness', together with the idea of inner wildernesses as well as physical ones.

Now, take five minutes to share any questions, observations or reflections that you have been thinking about the theme of wilderness this week

Turning to this week

This week we will be thinking about becoming the messengers of God's comfort.

As a group, share some experiences of those occasions when you have had really good news to tell:

- Whom did you tell?
- How did you do it?
- How did you feel about sharing the news?

Hearing the word   5 minutes

Ask someone in the group to read out the passage: Isaiah 40.6-11.

v. 6	A voice says 'Announce something,' and I said 'What shall I announce?'
	All living beings are grass and their steadfast love is like the blossom of the fields.
v. 7	Grass dries up and blossoms droop when the Spirit of God blows on it. The people are truly like grass.
v. 8	Grass withers and the blossom droops but the word of the Lord stands for eternity.
v. 9	Go up to a high mountain, Zion, bringer of good news; lift up your voice powerfully, Jerusalem, bringer of good news.
	Lift it up, don't be afraid, say to the cities of Judah: 'Look, your God'.
v. 10	Look, the Lord God is coming with strength, his arm rules for him; look his reward is with him and his wages are before him.
v. 11	He tends his flock like a shepherd, he gathers the lambs, he lifts them to his bosom and leads the mother sheep.

Word highlights

- **v. 6** – The word that I have translated 'announce' in is the generic word for making a sound and can mean cry out, call, proclaim. It could almost have been translated as: 'Make a sound,' and I said 'What kind of sound?'

  The word I have translated as 'steadfast love' is the word *hesed*, used often of the covenant relationship between God and his people. The word describes God's utterly abiding love for his people; in contrast, our steadfast love is like blossom, good while it lasts but easily blown away. This contrasts with God's word, which lasts for ever and ever.

- **v. 7** – In both Hebrew and Greek the same word is used for wind or breath as for spirit. Wind or breath is probably a better translation here but it is worth just using the word spirit to see if it makes any difference to how we think about the passage.

People highlights

One of the slightly confusing things about this passage is working out who God is addressing here. It may help you to know that scholars are not agreed about it.

1. Some think it is the inhabitants of Jerusalem and Judah who never went into exile.

2. Some think it is the exiles away in Babylon.

3. And some, of course, think it is both of them.

This passage (vv. 6-9) is where the real confusion arises. Until this point in Isaiah 40, it seems as though God is addressing the exiles (i.e. the people in Babylon) and getting them ready for return, but here he seems to be speaking to people who can go into the hill county of Judah and speak to the people who live there.

It is up to you to decide which of the options you think is right.

In my view the third option is a good possibility and God is addressing all those associated with Jerusalem and Judah who either live there now or used to live there before the exile. God sees the future for the whole city and nation, those away and those still back at home. All those associated with Jerusalem are to be involved with proclaiming God's message of good news that God, all powerful and all loving, is on his way.

Exploring the word

Finding and offering comfort

Ask someone to read out this short parable written by F. A. Krummacher in the nineteenth century:

> In the holy land lived a man called Eliab, whom God had blessed with earthly goods. He was also cunning in all the wisdom of the East. But all this could not bring peace to his heart; he was often full of sorrow and wished to die.
>
> Then a man of God came to him, and showed him an herb possessed of wonderful powers of healing; but Eliab said: 'What is that to me? My body lacks not health; my soul is diseased. It were better for me to die.' 'The herb will do thy heart good,' said the man of God. 'Take it, and heal seven sick men and then thou mayest die if thou wilt.' Eliab did as he was desired, and sought out misery in its abiding-places. He healed seven sick people and succoured the poor with his riches. Then the man of God came again to him and said, 'Here is an herb of death; now thou mayest die.' But Eliab cried: 'God forbid! My soul longeth no more for death, for now I comprehend the meaning and use of life.'
>
> *F. A. Krummacher*

Spend five minutes or so discussing the parable.

- Why do you think that Eliab no longer wanted to die at the end of parable?
- What do you think was 'the meaning and use of life' that Eliab felt he understood?

Comfort and experience

Both the parable we have just looked at and Isaiah 40.6-11 seem to say that people in need of comfort can be helped by offering comfort to others. This is not all that happens.

Sometimes those who are going through a bad time (or have been there recently) can offer profoundly effective comfort to those around them. In Isaiah 40.6-11, Isaiah is calling for the people of Jerusalem who have experienced a similar kind of grief to that of the cities of Judah to be the ones who pick up the message and announce it to their neighbours. It may be, indeed, that their own experience is what makes the comfort they bring even more effective than it would have been otherwise.

Of course it isn't always the case that those who feel despairing can reach out to others and bring comfort. There are occasions when people trying to do that end up simply talking about themselves and their own problems and ignoring the concerns of the person to whom they are talking. Sometimes we are so bogged down that we can no longer see straight and seem unable to reach beyond ourselves to help others.

'Don't look down on anyone, unless you are helping them up.'

Jesse Jackson

Some of us think holding on makes us strong; but sometimes it is letting go.

Herman Hesse

I waited patiently for the Lord;
he inclined to me and heard my cry.
He drew me up from the desolate pit,
out of the miry bog,
and set my feet upon a rock,
making my steps secure.

Psalm 40.1-2

Discuss one or more of the following questions:

- Why does shared experience help us to reach out more effectively to those around us?

- Think of occasions when someone has tried to comfort you and succeeded and also times when someone has tried and failed to comfort you. From your shared experiences try to work out what makes for an 'effective comforter' and an 'ineffective' comforter.

The presence of God

The message that Jerusalem must proclaim in this passage is that the God of might (v.10) and of tender care (v.11) is coming. The recipients of this message will not yet have seen any evidence of this. Those in exile will still be in exile; those who live in the ruins of Jerusalem will still live in ruins. Their message is to be that, seen or unseen, felt or unfelt, God is coming. Jerusalem must proclaim God's presence in faith, based upon what is already known about God and who he is rather than, necessarily, what they can see right now.

It is easy to feel downhearted about feeling close to God. Some people seem to feel God's presence all the time, while others go for weeks, months and even years between experiences of God's presence. Recently published letters from Mother Teresa indicate that this most holy woman went through times of feeling cut off from God and yet she carried on proclaiming God's presence in the care she expressed.

> Jesus has a very special love for you. As for me, the silence and the emptiness is so great that I look and do not see, listen and do not hear.
>
> *Mother Teresa to the Revd Michael Van Der Peet,*
> *September 1979*

> In prayer the deepest problem is not the absence of God but the absence of me.
>
> *Rowan Williams*

When you are disturbed, do not sin; ponder it on your beds, and be silent.
Offer right sacrifices, and put your trust in the Lord.
There are many who say, 'O that we might see some good! Let the light of your face shine on us, O Lord!'
You have put gladness in my heart more than when their grain and wine abound.

Psalm 4.4-7

Discuss one or more of the following questions:

● How do we proclaim God's presence when we simply do not feel it for ourselves?

● How helpful is it to be honest with others if we are going through a dry patch and not feeling God's presence in our lives right now? Should we admit this or keep it to ourselves?

Praying the word   5 minutes

It may be that you wish to spend more time on prayer and less time on the following task. If you find yourself short of time, invite people to begin to think about the task in the group and to finish it at home.

Spend a few moments calling to mind the people you know (or know of) who are most in need of prayer at the moment. Then move on to pray for them in silence or out loud, committing them to the love of God.

If your group is used to praying for people together, then pray as you normally do but, if not, it can be helpful to invite people simply to say out loud the name of the person or circumstance for which they wish to pray.

Reflecting and acting on the word

10 minutes

With some music playing, take an envelope and piece of paper or card and think of someone who particularly needs to hear the good news of God's presence at the moment.

Either:

● write them a short note, which you post or take to them after the group (it may be that you only start this now and finish it later when you have more time)

Or:

● write their name on the piece of paper and undertake to find some way, during the week, to encourage them with the assurance of God's love and presence.

Closing

5 minutes

The third aspect of God's help in a time of crisis to which Isaiah draws our attention is the need for us to become messengers of his comfort.

Write down something that you want to take away. It might be a quote, something someone said or something you want to think about some more.

As an end to your session, pray the following words together, ending with the prayer on the next page.

The person leading this part (who doesn't need to be the group leader) should say the words in regular type and the group should say the words in bold:

God of all comfort
Help us to become messengers of your love
In joy and in sorrow
Help us to become messengers of your love
When we feel your presence
Help us to become messengers of your love
When all we feel is abandoned and alone
Help us to become messengers of your love
As we seek to share your love with those around us
Help us to become messengers of your love
In all that we do
Help us to become messengers of your love,

Amen .

May the Lord bless us and keep us;
may the Lord make his face to shine upon us,
and be gracious to us;
may the Lord lift up his countenance upon us,
and give us peace.

Amen.

There is a lovely arrangement of this blessing by John Rutter (available on a number of different CDs or from the Internet as a sound file). If you have easy access to it, you may like to play it instead of simply saying the prayer.

At the end of the prayer – if you lit a candle blow it out to signal the end of the group.

4

Encountering God

At a glance

Getting started (15 minutes)

Opening prayer
Recap on last week
Thinking about the wonder of creation

Hearing the word (5 minutes)

Isaiah 40.21-26
Word highlights – a few explanations about the passage

Exploring the word (45–50 minutes)

Reflections, quotations and suggestions for group discussion focusing on:
● God the creator and us
● can we understand God?

Praying, reflecting and acting on the word (15 minutes)

Reflect on God's creation, and give thanks for all God has done for us

Closing (5 minutes)

Time to reflect on what you want to take away from the session
Closing prayer

Encountering God

Getting ready

To prepare for the session, you need to read the passage for study (Isaiah 40.21-26) and the reflection on the passage below. We recommend that all group members read the reflection to help them focus their thoughts on the topic for this session but, if people don't have the time to do this, they will still be able to take part in the discussion.

More on Isaiah 40.21-26

There is a cartoon, that I had on a birthday card once, featuring two grasshoppers sitting on a leaf looking up at the sky and saying: 'It kinda makes you feel insignificant doesn't it?'. The point of the cartoon is that the grasshoppers not only feel small and quite insignificant, they are small and quite insignificant – the implication is that we might well be small and insignificant too. There is something about the sheer scale, variety and beauty of creation that not only takes the breath away but also reminds us of how small we are in the scheme of things. Looking at the stars, seeing the view from the top of a mountain or walking along a beach can all remind us of how insignificant we really are.

What, you may be wondering, has realizing our own insignificance got to do with God's help in a time of crisis? Surely realizing our own smallness is only going to make us feel worse rather than better? Isaiah seems to think not, because his song of praise of God's greatness as creator goes on for much longer than any other section in this chapter. His point here, however, is not so much about reminding us how small we are, but about how great God is. The sky, which to us is vast and immeasurable, was created by God with as little effort as we might use to close a curtain or put up a tent. It all depends on your perspective. What are for us the most enormous, challenging and insurmountable aspects of the created world – like, for example, Mount Everest – can be picked up and weighed on scales by God.

Encountering this God can bring comfort. If the highest mountain can be picked up by God to be weighed and if the deepest sea can be measured in his hand, then our problems that feel far too vast for us to handle are similarly small to God. What we can barely lift can be tossed aside like an ant for God. This doesn't belittle the enormity of what we go through, but it does mean that there is someone for whom our problems are not impossible.

Possibly the most amazing part of Isaiah's message in this chapter is that we, like the grasshoppers of the cartoon, may feel insignificant in the face of the world that God has created, but we are not. The God who can scoop up the oceans in his hand is also the God who, in verse 1, sought to comfort his people. Before the incredible greatness of God, we should, really, be as important as grasshoppers; instead we are people whom God loves, cares for and cherishes. Looking up to the skies may make us feel insignificant but it should also remind us that the God who made the world and everything in it, loves us and yearns to comfort us.

Things you will need for the group

- A candle
- Some music to play
- Music-playing equipment
- Something for each member of the group to have that will communicate the wonder of creation (e.g. flowers, pine cones, shells, etc. but *not* a feather as you will need one of these next week). You can choose either all the same thing or a variety of different things and allow the group to choose what they want to take away

Encountering God

Getting started

Opening prayer

Light a candle, then open the study with the course prayer – either use this one or one of your own.

> God of all comfort,
> where we are stuck, release us,
> where we have given up hope, inspire us,
> where we focus only on ourselves,
> help us to see the needs of others;
> transform us by your Spirit to be the people you have called us to be,
> spreading your love and proclaiming your presence throughout the world.
> We ask this through your son,
> our Saviour Jesus Christ.
> Amen.

Recap on last week

Last week's session reminded us of our own role as messengers of God's comfort to the world around us.

Take five minutes to share any questions, observations or reflections that you have been thinking about the theme of becoming God's messengers this week.

Turning to this week

For each one of us, the wonder of creation is crystallized by different things. For some people it is expressed in the vastness of the night sky, for others in the intricate detail of a flower's petal.

Share with the group what part of the world around most communicates the wonder of God's creation to you.

Hearing the word

Ask someone in the group to read out the passage: Isaiah 40.21-26 (this section of Isaiah 40 is longer than all the others. You may like to read just the short bit included below or you can explore the whole passage, which runs from verse 12 to verse 26).

v. 21 Don't you know? Haven't you heard? Hasn't it been declared to you from the beginning? Haven't you discerned from the foundations of the earth?

v. 22 He is the one who sits above the earth's sky (and the earth's inhabitants are like grasshoppers).

He stretches out the heavens like a curtain and spreads them like a tent to live in.

v. 23 He gives princes into nothingness and makes judges into emptiness.

v. 24 Barely have they been planted, barely have they been sown, barely has their stem taken root in the earth, when he blows on them and they shrivel; the tempest carries them off like chaff.

v. 25 'Who do you compare me to that I should be equal?' says the Holy One.

v. 26 Lift up your eyes up and look at the skies. Who created these?

He brings out their army in number, calling them all by name; because of his abundant strength and might not one is missing.

Word highlights

● **v. 22** – The words used for 'curtain' and 'tent' are ordinary everyday words and are designed to emphasize that what is for us an act of mind-blowing splendour was for God as easy as opening a curtain.

● **v. 23** – The word I have translated as 'emptiness' is the same word that is used in the Genesis 1 creation story for how the world was before God began creation (the NRSV translates this as 'formless' and the NIV as 'empty'). In other words, in reducing the great and good of the day to 'emptiness', God makes the most important things in our world empty and pointless.

Exploring the word

God the creator and us

One of the recurring themes of the Old Testament is that of God's power as creator and our relationship to him. In twos or threes, or in the group as a whole, spend some time looking at the following passages alongside our main passage, Isaiah 40.21-26.

When I look at your heavens, the work of your fingers,
the moon and the stars that you have established;
what are human beings that you are mindful of them,
mortals that you care for them?
Yet you have made them a little lower than God,
and crowned them with glory and honour.

Psalm 8.3-5

Long ago you laid the foundation of the earth,
and the heavens are the work of your hands.
They will perish, but you endure;
they will all wear out like a garment.
You change them like clothing, and they pass away;
but you are the same, and your years have no end.

Psalm 102.25-27

Thus says God, the Lord, who created the heavens and stretched them out, who spread out the earth and what comes from it, who gives breath to the people upon it and spirit to those who walk in it: I am the Lord, I have called you in righteousness, I have taken you by the hand and kept you; I have given you as a covenant to the people, a light to the nations.

Isaiah 42.5-6

Discuss the following question. From the passages above, when the Old Testament writers look at creation, what conclusions do they draw:

- about God?

- about us?

- and about our relationship with God?

If you discussed this in twos and threes, spend some time sharing your ideas in the group as a whole; when you have done that move on to the questions below.

Throughout the Old Testament, people seem to have found comfort in an acknowledgement of the wonder and majesty of God as creator.

- What is it, do you think, that helped them? Does it help you?

- Is there anything about it that is not helpful?

> All I have seen teaches me to trust the Creator for all I have not seen.
> *Ralph Waldo Emerson*

> Some people, in order to discover God, read books. But there is a great book: the very appearance of created things. Look above you! Look below you! Read it. God, whom you want to discover, never wrote that book with ink. Instead he set before your eyes the things that he had made. Can you ask for a louder voice than that?
> *St Augustine*

> Have courage for the great sorrows of life and patience for the small ones; and when you have laboriously accomplished your daily task, go to sleep in peace. God is awake.
> *Victor Hugo*

Can we understand God?

There is another theme connected to this both in Isaiah 40.21-26 and in a number of other Old Testament passages. Probably the clearest expression of it can be found in the book of Job. Job was afflicted with all sorts of suffering (his children were killed, his livelihood taken away, his health was in tatters), and much of the book is taken up with a long discussion between Job and his rather unsympathetic friends about why this has happened to him. Right at the end of the book, God spoke to Job out of a whirlwind and said that Job cannot understand the world and why things happen because, unlike God, he did not create it. See below for a short sample of the kind of language used:

> Who is this that darkens counsel by words without knowledge? Gird up your loins like a man, I will question you, and you shall declare to me.
>
> 'Where were you when I laid the foundation of the earth? Tell me, if you have understanding. Who determined its measurements – surely you know! Or who stretched the line upon it? On what were its bases sunk, or who laid its cornerstone when the morning stars sang together and all the heavenly beings shouted for joy?
>
> *Job 38.2-7*

After his encounter with God, Job seemed to agree with God and acknowledged that he did not understand how the world worked (Job 42.3 'I have uttered what I did not understand, things too wonderful for me, which I did not know.'). His encounter with God and his recognition that God was a creator beyond his comprehension seemed to satisfy his agonizing about suffering and why he had suffered.

....

The question of suffering and how to respond to it is, probably, one of the hardest questions that Christians have to face. Acknowledging, then, that it is unlikely you will solve it today, explore the following questions together:

● How might acknowledging that we cannot understand the world as God does help us to come to terms with suffering?

● Do you find it an adequate response to the problem of suffering?

....

If the Lord Almighty had consulted me before embarking upon Creation, I should have recommended something simpler.

Alfonso X of Castile

It takes both sunshine and rain to make a rainbow.

Author unknown

O Lord, my heart is not lifted up, my eyes are not raised too high; I do not occupy myself with things too great and too marvellous for me. But I have calmed and quieted my soul, like a weaned child with its mother; my soul is like the weaned child that is with me. O Israel, hope in the Lord from this time on and forevermore.

Psalm 131.1-3

Praying, reflecting and acting on the word

15 minutes

While the music plays, hold in your hand a symbol of creation (shell, pine cone, flower or something similar) given to you by the group leader. Use it to focus your thoughts on creation and the God who has created it:*

*If you have time, and your group would appreciate it, you might at this point like to be even more creative.

- For example, you could give the group pencil and paper and encourage them to spend some time drawing the detail of what they see before them or to write down the words that occur to them as they look at the item they hold.

- Alternatively you could give a slide show on a laptop (or any other way!), which contains pictures of creation.

After five minutes or so, move into a time of prayer in which you give thanks for the world that God has created and commit to the care of creator God the troubles of the world he has created.

The group might prefer to pray freely but if they find it helpful they might like to gather prayers under the following headings. The group leader can introduce each section with the words below:

We give thanks for the world that God has created:

(In this section you might like to thank God for general aspects of creation – running streams, trees, etc. or for particular places where you feel especially close to God.)

We give thanks to God for all he has given to us:

(In this section you might like to thank God for those gifts that you experience in your life – love of family and/or friends, etc.)

We bring to God those things that trouble the world he has created:

(In this section you can be as wide ranging or specific as you like, praying for conflict, natural disasters or people known to you who are suffering.)

At the end of this session, take with you the symbol of creation that you were given and use it to remind you to give thanks to God for the world he has created every day this week.

Closing   5 minutes

The fourth aspect of God's help in a time of crisis to which Isaiah draws our attention is the need for us to encounter the God who created our world and so see ourselves as he sees us.

Write down something that you want to take away. It might be a quote, something someone said or something you want to think about some more.

As an end to your session, pray the following words together, ending with the prayer below.

The person leading this part (who doesn't need to be the group leader) should say the words in regular type and the group should say the words in bold:

When we look at the world you have made

We praise your name, O God

When we think about all that you have done

We praise your name, O God

When we remember what you have done for us

We praise your name, O God

In the good times and the bad

We praise your name, O God

In trust, for all the future holds

We praise your name, O God. Amen.

End your prayers with the words of this favourite hymn. If you are going to say it (rather than sing it) the leader of the prayers can say the words in regular type and the group the words in bold.

O Lord my God! when I in awesome wonder
consider all the works thy hand hath made,
I see the stars, I hear the mighty thunder,
thy power throughout the universe displayed:

Then sings my soul, my Saviour God, to thee:
how great thou art! How great thou art!

Amen.

continued on p. 60

Of course you may prefer to sing it, in which case the words for the whole hymn are below or, if you have easy access to a recorded copy of it, you could play that while people reflect on the words.

O Lord my God, when I in awesome wonder
consider all the works thy hand hath made,
I see the stars, I hear the mighty thunder,
thy power throughout the universe displayed:

Then sings my soul, my Saviour God, to thee:
how great thou art! How great thou art!

When through the woods and forest glades I wander
and hear the birds sing sweetly in the trees;
when I look down on lofty mountain grandeur,
and hear the brook, and feel the gentle breeze.

And when I think that God his Son not sparing,
Sent him to die – I scarce can take it in.
That on the cross my burden gladly bearing,
he bled and died to take away my sin.

When Christ shall come with shout of acclamation
and take me home – what joy shall fill my heart!
Then shall I bow in humble adoration
and there proclaim, my God, how great thou art!

By Stuart K. Hine
copyright © 1953 The Stuart Hine Trust/kingswaysongs.com

At the end of the prayer – if you lit a candle, blow it out to signal the end of the group.

5

Receiving fresh strength

At a glance

Getting started (15 minutes)

Opening prayer
Recap on last week
Thinking about recharging our batteries

Hearing the word (5 minutes)

The passage: Isaiah 40.27-31
Word highlights – a few explanations about the passage

Exploring the word (40–45 minutes)

Reflections, quotations and suggestions for group discussion focusing on:
- waiting for God
- mounting up on wings like eagles

Reflecting on the word (5 minutes)

Spend time reflecting on your need for God's strength

Praying the word and acting on the word (5–10 minutes)

Focus on waiting for the Lord, prayer for those in need of renewal of
  strength and undertaking to wait more consciously for the Lord
  in the week to come

Looking to the future (5 minutes)

Time to reflect on what you have learnt and what you want to take
  with you to reflect on further

Closing (5 minutes)

Closing prayer

5 Receiving fresh strength

Getting ready

To prepare for the session, you need to read the passage for study (Isaiah 40.27-31) and the reflection on the passage below. We recommend that all group members read the reflection to help them focus their thoughts on the topic for this session but, if people don't have the time to do this, they will still be able to take part in the discussion.

More on Isaiah 40.27-31

There is something captivating about the flight of eagles. I'll never forget as a child coming over the brow of a hill, on a walk with my parents and sister, and coming across a golden eagle. For a fraction of a second, it carried on walking – lumbering around on ungainly feet – before soaring, effortlessly, into the sky. In fact one of the most enchanting features of eagles is the contrast between their awkward walk and graceful flight: it is hard to imagine that anything as ungainly as an eagle on the ground could transform into something as graceful as an eagle in flight.

This is one of the reasons why Isaiah's image here at the end of chapter 40 is so inspirational. Verses 27-30 speak profoundly of the reality of our human existence, which is so often marked by weariness. The grind of daily life, of simply keeping going when we are exhausted, can be hard enough at the best of times but becomes even harder when we are in the midst of a crisis of whatever kind. As Isaiah says in verse 30, even the young who are strong and full of energy get tired and worn down, but God does not. The Lord is the God of eternity (v. 28) whose strength knows no limits. This is the God who seeks us to comfort us and give us new strength.

With a few well chosen words, Isaiah communicates to us in 40.27-31 the current emotions of the people to whom he is speaking as well as an inspirational vision for the future. The people are lost, alone and exhausted. Although he does not make it explicit, I think what he is describing here is what it is like to have been lost in the wilderness. The people have gone on for as long as they can but now they have run out of strength – to use a word that Isaiah uses of the young in verse 30, they have completely fallen over or collapsed – and in their despair they fear that God, wearied by the search, will be unable to find them and will pass by without noticing where they are. In other words they fear that the rescue party has come out to look for them but can't find them.

It is in this context that Isaiah reminds us that the God in whom we believe never runs out of energy nor gets tired. This God is indefatigable and will never give up. In response, we are to keep on looking out for God. The word used can be translated as 'wait' but this has a passive edge to it that I'm not sure is meant here. We are not called to hang around passively waiting for God to turn up but to focus our eyes on the distance, looking out for God and, hence, recognizing him when he comes. Once when I was waiting for a bus, I became so caught up in my own thoughts that the bus came and went and only as it pulled off did I realize that I had missed it (while standing at the bus stop!). There is a danger that we can do the same with God: we get so caught up in our own concerns that we don't even notice the action and comfort of God when it is offered to us. Those who wait actively for God, Isaiah tells us, will not only recognize him when he is in their midst but will find themselves transformed by God's own strength. As a result they will no longer lumber around exhausted and weary but take to the wing, rising up with the grace and beauty of an eagle in flight.

Things you will need for the group

- A candle
- Either a flip chart and pens or a large piece of paper
- Some music to play
- Music-playing equipment
- A feather (either see if you can find enough outside for the group or go to a children's craft shop or area where you can buy packs of multi-coloured feathers quite cheaply)

Receiving fresh strength

Getting started

15 minutes

Opening prayer

Light a candle, then open the study with the course prayer – either use this one or one of your own.

God of all comfort,
where we are stuck, release us,
where we have given up hope, inspire us,
where we focus only on ourselves,
help us to see the needs of others;
transform us by your Spirit to be the people
you have called us to be,
spreading your love and proclaiming your
presence throughout the world.
We ask this through your son,
our Saviour Jesus Christ.
Amen.

Recap on last week

Last week's session explored the idea of encountering the God who created the world and how this might help us in the midst of life's sufferings.

Take five minutes to share any questions, observations or reflections that you have been thinking about the theme of encountering God this week.

Turning to this week

When you get absolutely exhausted, what do you do to recharge your batteries?

Share with the group as a whole what kinds of thing begin to make you feel better when you are very tired.

Hearing the word

5 minutes

Ask someone in the group to read out the passage: Isaiah 40.27-31.

v. 27	Why do you say, Jacob and speak, Israel: 'My path is concealed from the Lord and justice from my God has passed by'?
v. 28	Have you not known? Have you not heard? The Lord is the God of eternity who creates the ends of the earth. He does not exhaust himself fruitlessly nor does he get tired by working. There is no searching out of his understanding.
v. 29	He gives to the exhausted the ability to go on and for those without strength he increases their might.
v. 30	Even the young get exhausted and young men get tired by working; they collapse.
v. 31	Those who look out for the Lord will renew their strength, they will go up on wings like eagles, they will run and not get tired; they will walk and not get exhausted.

Word highlights

- **v. 27** – This opens with a vivid image of rescue. God's people seem to believe that they are on a path in the wilderness that God cannot find. So, in his attempt to rescue them and bring them justice, he passes by and doesn't notice where they are. Isaiah points out that this is not the case: God will not miss them and never gets tired in his searching.

- **v. 28** – The two words for getting tired are evocative. The first has the sense of wearing yourself out by doing something that you cannot achieve and the second of getting tired by toiling away at your work. God does neither of these but human beings do.

- **v. 30** – Isaiah uses the same two words for getting tired as in v. 28, to show that even the young get tired whereas God does not.

  The word that I have translated as 'collapse' means literally to fall or stumble badly.

Exploring the word

You will need to take slightly less time today for your discussion as, since this is the last session, there is more to do at the end.

Waiting for God

Waiting around and waiting for

Waiting can easily be seen as passing the time away between one event and another. It can become dead time with no great purpose to it other than that we wait for something to happen. This does not seem to be what Isaiah means here. The whole of Isaiah 40 has been about the active expectation of God's presence, which will come and transform us. The same seems to be true here. In fact, the word used by Isaiah in verse 31 has overtones of being a look-out, straining to see whatever is coming in the far distance.

Sometimes when we're waiting for God to speak, He's waiting for us to listen.

Martha Bolton

All things come to him who waits – provided he knows what he is waiting for.

Woodrow T. Wilson

Waiting for God is not laziness. Waiting for God is not going to sleep. Waiting for God is not the abandonment of effort.

G. Campbell Morgan

God waits like a beggar who stands motionless and silent before someone who will perhaps give him a piece of bread. Time is that waiting. Time is God's waiting for our love ... By waiting humbly we are made similar to God.

Simone Weil, in George A. Panicha (ed.), The Simone Weil Reader, *David McKay Company, 1977*

Spend some time exploring the difference in attitude between passively waiting around and actively waiting for something.

Either:

- Imagine two people. One of them is waiting around for nothing in particular; the other is actively waiting for something (like, for example, a bus).

- Discuss what might characterize the difference in their attitude and behaviour.

- What would you look out for that might tell you what kind of waiting they were doing?

Or:

- Put two columns on a large piece of paper or flip chart (one headed 'waiting around' and the other headed 'waiting for') and write down the words/emotions that you might associate with each one.

Or, indeed, you could do a combination of both.

Waiting for the Lord

Holding this in mind, now go on to talk about waiting for God and what it means in practice. Waiting for God is one of those ideas that sounds good but can be hard to put into practice.

Discuss one or more of the following questions:

- Using the words and ideas you associated with 'waiting for', discuss what attitudes you might adopt if you were waiting for God.

- In addition to adopting a certain attitude, what kinds of thing might you do in practice if you were consciously 'waiting for the Lord'?

  - How might this affect the way in which you pray?

  - Would it affect any other part of your life as well as your prayer life?

- Think back to moments in your life when you felt conscious that you were waiting for God? How did it affect what you did?

Mounting up on wings like eagles

One of the things that becomes very clear in Isaiah 40.27-31 is that human strength – even that of the young – is fickle and fades easily, but that God's strength goes on for ever and ever. If we are to soar like eagles, then, we need God's strength and not our own to do it. In reality many of us would be content simply to keep going: forget soaring like eagles, just getting through the day can sometimes feel hard enough. Yet God constantly seeks to give us his strength, a strength that is far greater than our minds can even imagine.

Surely God is my salvation; I will trust, and will not be afraid, for the Lord God is my strength and my might; he has become my salvation.

Isaiah 12.2

Let God's promises shine on your problems.

Corrie Ten Boom

God's gifts put your dreams to shame.

Elizabeth Barrett Browning

Discuss one or more of the following questions:

- Mounting up on wings like eagles, running and not getting tired and walking and never getting exhausted are powerful images that evoke a range of thoughts and feelings. What vision do they give you of what your life could be like?

- Have you ever felt supported by God's strength rather than your own? If you feel able to, share with the group what this was like for you.

Reflecting on the word · 5 minutes

While music plays, in silence hold in your hand a feather given to you by the group leader.

- Focus your thoughts and prayers on those aspects of your life for which you most need God's strength at present.

- Commit yourself to waiting for God's presence and strength to carry you through.

Praying the word · 5–10 minutes

As a group, turn outwards in your prayers and pray especially for those people (or groups of people) known to you who are themselves in particular need of renewal of strength at the moment.

Acting on the word · 1 minute

Take your feather home and put it somewhere that will remind you to re-focus yourself towards waiting for God and receiving the strength that he gives. You might like to make a resolution to spend five minutes each day for the next week actively waiting for God.

Looking to the future · 5 minutes

Over the course of these five sessions we have explored five aspects of Isaiah's message that enable us to understand more about the help God offers in a time of crisis. Like self-help, each one of these requires us to do something:

1 Embrace comfort

2 Step out into the wilderness

3 Become messengers

4 Encounter God

5 Receive fresh strength

... but, unlike self-help, they do not require us to do it alone.

Spend a few minutes reflecting on the five aspects that we have explored. You might like to make a note of something that you feel you have learnt that you wish to take away, or something(s) that you wish to think about further as you journey onwards with God.

Closing

As an end to your session, pray the following words together, ending with the prayer below.

The person leading this part (who doesn't need to be the group leader) should say the words in regular type and the group should say the words in bold:

> As we journey onwards from this place
>
> **Give us your strength, O Lord**
>
> As we face life's trials
>
> **Give us your strength, O Lord**
>
> As we comfort others in their suffering
>
> **Give us your strength, O Lord**
>
> As we seek to spread your love throughout the world
>
> **Give us your strength, O Lord**
>
> That we might mount up on wings like eagles
>
> **Amen.**

May the strength of God pilot us,
may the wisdom of God instruct us,
may the hand of God protect us,
may the word of God direct us.
Be always ours this day and for evermore.

Amen.

A Blessing of St Patrick

At the end of the prayer – if you lit a candle blow it out to signal the end of the group.